Quantump

Rosana Kibby Cox

Illustrations by Emma Crooks

Copyright © 2023 Rosana Kibby Cox

All rights reserved.

ISBN: 978-84-09-50459-6

For Evan

There is one illustration in this book that invites you to complete it. This book is also available as a hardback in sketch book format. With additional drawings and including incomplete artwork to get you started, embedded writing exercises along with additional blank pages, it's a book of poems offering space for your own creative inspirations.

Quantumplate That

A collection of poems titled...

They are asking to be read by you

In this realm of reality

Let us set us free

Worn by you with a feeling of ease

We do hold the power to fix all that is wrong

Tending to thoughts that run dark and deep

Built on a false that cannot last

Taken again by the sight of your light

And in all us others too

Thank you for playing the way you play

Sing a vista through this misty veil

But we did it anyway

Wonderfully we

Author´s note

They are asking to be read by you

Rhymes are good and rhymes are sweet

Some make you move your hands and your feet

They have a rhythm and a flow

Can teach you things you did not know

Rhymes can be fast or rhymes can be slow

Some stay with you as you grow

They might change shape and miss a line

But some will stand the test of time

Rhymes are bright and rhymes can chime

Some tell a story of sadness that feels like it's mine

They can drive a pace or hold a beat

Can reach in places cold and deep

And warm them just by describing heat

Rhymes have highs and rhymes have lows

Some lift you up, others deliver blows

They can do both or neither, but still stir some change

Engaging minds with the pattern of words they arrange

Rhymes said alone or rhymes said on a stage

Asking to be lifted from a page

Sometimes fantasy sometimes true

They are asking to be read by you

In this realm of reality

I am a being of immense complexity

In me lies the breadth and width of infinity

An expression of a love so strong I hold density

An explosion of endless energy

Part of an intricate web of inter-connectivity

Powerful beyond quantifiable measurability

Bound to a form so you will recognise me

In this realm of reality

Let us set us free

I fantasise about a mother divine,

I am hers and she is mine

Our hearts and souls are intertwined

And life feels soft and fine

Then, in a glitch she slips from my grip

A switch trips, and

I fumble for her in the dark

I thumb at where she's left her mark

Stumbling through a life left stark

It feels cold and sharp

I call out but my voice sounds a raspy bark

I fall and there she is to catch me

Always Tierra, there beneath me

Reminded by each step so briefly

Reminded with each breath that fills me

Always cosmos that surrounds me

It astounds me, how could I forget?

When was the moment that we met?

Mother nature is all around

Not all statements are made with sound

She shows me something pure and true

Something I already knew

"I am you and you are me,"

"I am not a fantasy."

Divinity unravels time

Reality is not a line

I am her and she is me

And that is how we grew this tree

The family

Humanity

Let us set us free

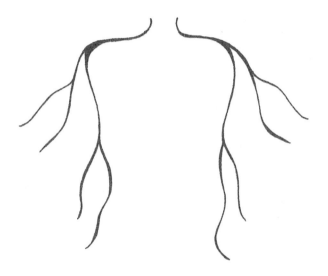

Worn by you with a feeling of ease

Wear life like a loose fitting garment

Let it not weigh you down

Cause you to frown

Or get lost and drown

Let it not constrict

Too tight a fit

A feeling you are in its grip

But not too loose that it might slip

Wear your life garment with pride

It's yours to wear and it would be wise

Not to let others climb inside

Not too narrow, too wide

And not a place in which to hide

Let it make you feel a glow

Have a smooth swish and a rhythmic flow

Leave you space in which to grow

Make you want to dance with others that you know

Let it empower you to frame

A life in which you feel no shame

It need not sparkle, it can be plain

But let it serve you joy not pain

Wear your life garment while you're here

Make adjustments with each passing year

Offer it love, air out any clouds of fear

What needs updating will be clear

Let it age with tending grace

This light fitting garment that is your soul, and your face

Slip your arms into soft sleeves

Let them flutter in the breeze

Worn by you with a feeling of ease

We do hold the power to fix all that is wrong

A call to arms

Fire the alarms

Protect the farms

Pool together all lucky charms

Time to settle all our qualms

No time to wait

Or hesitate

Or just sit back and call it fate

The tide is turning

The seas are churning

History around us is unfurling

But really, it's just a few men, earning

They're earning, while mankind is yearning

They're earning from the things they're burning

Dining on the things they're mining

Making from the things they're taking

Dancing on the things they're chancing

Of course these things belong to us

But we are too polite to make a fuss

Too uptight to voice our right

Too do distracted to realise our power

But hear the plea this is the hour

The milk of Mother Earth is turning sour

We've been divided distracted, confused and misused

But now is the moment we have to choose

You know the phrase, you snooze you loose

Nature is reeling

We are all feeling

Coming together in a collective healing

Come on let us stand together and unite

Step out of the dark and into the light

If you have gone on a journey come back tonight

If you somehow manage to live in the now

Together we all must lift our gaze

Our footsteps show us we have strayed

Possibly we can say it is just a phase

In our attempts to get back we've built a maze

But the power of human intention is strong

We do hold a power to fix all that is wrong

Tending to thoughts that run dark and deep

There is a veil that masks the bright

Struggling with shadows I should embrace not fight

Entangled with a sense of fright

Following paths as if a pilgrim

Ascending submits in search of healing

Finding truth in my unreeling

The trickle of the falling water

It knows its way it does not falter

These mountain tops they are an altar

I am

Reflected in their varied faces

Hidden in their many places

Mirrored in their shifting gazes

Though they are so harsh and steep

In their embrace I feel safe to weep

As I tend to those thoughts that run dark and deep

Built on a false that cannot last

I used to think that there was time

Space energy and matter

And that was fine

I was taught that things were set

Water was always H2o

The universe had clear rules it met

This is just to name a few

That now reveal the cheap poor glue

As now I find these things untrue

Along with many others too

Parts of our history and those firm dates

Now no longer resonate

And those things I was taught held no weight;

The World as myths and legends state

That there is a clear distinction

Between stories labelled fact and fiction

The things we cheer and the things we fear

The feelings we hold and the truths we are told

Have an impact far and wide

Generate a reality in which we hide

From light and sounds so clear and true

Knowledge held both ancient and new

But in this place we cannot grow

The magnificence of our true colours barely show

In this dim glow

How can we know?

I sift through thoughts that flit and flail

Smothered by a stale and fading vale

They wish to sail

I found a moment and I sat

In stillness there is time to quantumplate that

That is beyond the curtain

Of what is certain

A dragonfly in iridescent glory

Reminds us of another story

As she darts past with precision grace

Wearing in pride an alien face

She reminds us the illusions we hold fast

Are built on a false that cannot last.

This was not an anti-science poem, but inspired by my love of quantum physics, space science, microbiology, archeology, and generally the shared human quest for understanding. I am against a scientific dogma that mirrors religious and other older dogmatic behaviour in that new ideas labelled as fringe receive no funding and are ridiculed instead of explored. Scientific discovery should be about exploring beyond the veil of what is certain, not filling pockets, massaging egos or staying on the right side of a predetermined hypothesis. Poems should be left to interpretation, so I've said too much.
p.s. Did you know water can be $H3O2$?

Taken again by the site of your light

I am a moth

Taken to flight

And also quite taken by the sight of your light

You draw me in towards your dazzle

Blinded and at risk of frazzle

You're hot to touch

I know that much

My fragile wings survive the same

I turn and there you are again

I am a moth

You are my light

I am a moth

I take to flight

Taken again by the sight

And in all us others too

You lift me up and drag me under

Churn me round in waves like thunder

Wrap me up in caves of wonder

In them are there are answers why

Then you spit me up up so high

When on your waves I take a leap

And in your depths your treasures seek

In your soft beds I soak and seep

And at those places where soft shore lines meet

I gently stroke at where the land and sea lap and greet

And slap at others where line's more stark

Leaving a much more jagged mark

Sometimes thrashing at sharp walls in the dark

Those high walls

My frustration that they exist at all

Only seems to build them tall

Leaving more places we could fall

But somehow in this place submerged

By elemental forces converged

At these places I can find the verge

Of an absolute calm

So full of power and safe from harm

Occasionally the sun will kiss

A still surface of a mirrored bliss

And from this place

A ripple sent

Can roll eternal

It's track unbent

While deep below, shared rivers flow

And as they grow

They show their signs

In ways traced out by their deep set lines

Light dances on the surface as their patterns shine

From this place of serenity

When it's calm comes clarity

Ancient wisdoms you held kept

Became so clear I almost wept

An infinity that lies in you

And in all us others too

Thank you for playing the way you play

(For my second son on his first birthday)

We met this day a year ago

Before I knew the things I now know

Those things you've taught me, they are many

I hope I have not taught you any

For the things that you already knew

Were the important ones that still hold true

Through this first year we've spent together

And all the storms we've had to weather

You've shown me there's a truth so sweet

The one we feel, as it tickles our hands and our feet

You remind me of another time

A fairer one when things were fine

And that, somehow, that time is now

Whenever I forget, or I'm feeling low

You remind me, eyes fixed in their fierce glow

It's not tomorrow, or yesterday

It's today

Thank you for playing the way you play

Sing a vista through this misty veil

I once sat out under a red moon

I held hands and hiked over sand dunes

Fell in love with a simple tune

And enjoyed the sweeping action of my broom

I found smooth rocks to hold

Listened to whispers of stories told

Both old and new,

Bold and true

And explored the places where they meet and fold

I felt the breeze

Ran my hand over the rustling leaves

Jumped high with a spring of ease

And took delight not fright with every sneeze

I strode out into a gale

And hoped for howling winds in which to flail

And swing and swish my every wish to derail

And sing a vista through this misty veil

But we did it anyway

Do you remember that time?

When we found a line arbitrarily drawn in the land

And we were told not to cross it

So we didn't

Do you remember that time?

When we were told that at we were different to each other

And some people were better

Do you remember that time?

When some people had it all

While others had not enough at all

Do you remember that time?

When we had lost our connection with seed

And we consumed food that fed no need

Except profit and greed

Do you remember that time?

When the climate raged

The ongoing destruction and ignoring of warnings

seemed like they were staged

When all of a sudden we lifted our gaze

We came out of our haze

We put things right

We found one another

We found mother nature

And we held her tight

Do you remember that time

When we found a line arbitrarily drawn in the land

And we were told not to cross it

But we did it anyway

Wonderfully we

We

We are

We are all

We are all equal

We are all equally powerful

We are all equally powerfully individual

We are all equally powerfully individually integral

We are all equally powerfully individually integrally intuitive

We are all equally powerfully individually integrally intuitively wild

We are all equally powerfully individually integrally intuitively wildly wise

We are all equally powerfully individually integrally intuitively wildly wisely wonderful

We are all equally powerfully individually integrally intuitively wildly wisely wonderfully we

We, and its power to include all of us should not be underestimated. We are all equally deserving of acknowledgement as a powerful intuitive offering, an aspect of the wilds wisdom, and making up an integral part of the wonderful that is we.

Wonderfully we

Author's note

I hope you enjoyed this arrangement of words into patterns and onto pages. It took a lot of convincing and confidence building for me to share the crazy place in my mind where everything rhymes and I want to thank all those who pushed me towards completing this project, friends, family and strangers at poetry nights, and Emma for doing such beautiful drawings. I hope that others who read this are encouraged to share their creative expressions.

I am based sometimes in South London UK, where I grew up, and more often in Las Alpujarras, Spain where I live, farm, take solo hikes, teach alternative economics, mum my four young boys and continually learn about anything and everything that I can. I perform spoken word, live music and poetry at ´Poetry for the People´; a movement and creative family to whom I express deep gratitude, for offering space for sharing words I needed to hear, and where I am honoured to feel heard.

I feel like I should thank more people, because gratitude is beautiful. Thank you to my Grandma June, for it is since you left that I trip into a time and space of rhyme and I can find those words that chime. Thank you to my supportive parents and I am grateful for my partner and children for being in my life everyday.

A final thank you to you for taking the time to read Quantumplate That, and consider what lies beyond the curtain of what is certain. May we feel a little bit less alone. Please feel free to read these words to any ears that you feel need to hear them. They are for sharing, they never belonged to me. I tuned a dail, words can transform, poems are transmitters, along with my voice and yours.

Dance more, music is what life is for.

I don't know why I wrote that but it came through

And it's true

So who knew?

Printed in Great Britain
by Amazon